Favorite Pets

Fish

by Christina Leaf

BLASTOFF!
Beginners

BELLWETHER MEDIA
MINNEAPOLIS, MN

Blastoff! Beginners are developed by literacy experts and educators to meet the needs of early readers. These engaging informational texts support young children as they begin reading about their world. Through simple language and high frequency words paired with crisp, colorful photos, Blastoff! Beginners launch young readers into the universe of independent reading.

Blastoff! Universe

Reading Level — Grade K

Grades 1-3

Grade 4

Sight Words in This Book 🔍

a	get	make	want
are	help	many	water
can	in	of	with
do	is	the	you
eat	it	there	
find	like	to	

This edition first published in 2021 by Bellwether Media, Inc.

No part of this publication may be reproduced in whole or in part without written permission of the publisher. For information regarding permission, write to Bellwether Media, Inc., Attention: Permissions Department, 6012 Blue Circle Drive, Minnetonka, MN 55343.

Library of Congress Cataloging-in-Publication Data

Names: Leaf, Christina, author.
Title: Fish / by Christina Leaf.
Description: Minneapolis, MN : Bellwether Media, Inc., 2021. | Series: Favorite pets |
   Includes bibliographical references and index. | Audience: Ages PreK-2 | Audience: Grades K-1
Identifiers: LCCN 2020007066 | ISBN 9781644873151 (library binding) | ISBN 9781681038025 (paperback) |
   ISBN 9781681037783 (ebook)
Subjects: LCSH: Fishes--Juvenile literature.
Classification: LCC QL617.2 .L43 2021 | DDC 598--dc23
LC record available at https://lccn.loc.gov/2020007066
Library of Congress Cataloging-in-Publication Data

Text copyright © 2021 by Bellwether Media, Inc. BLASTOFF! BEGINNERS and associated logos are trademarks and/or registered trademarks of Bellwether Media, Inc.

Editor: Amy McDonald   Designer: Jeffrey Kollock

Printed in the United States of America, North Mankato, MN.

Table of Contents

Pet Fish!

Do you want
a pretty pet?
Fish are colorful!

There are many
kinds of pet fish.

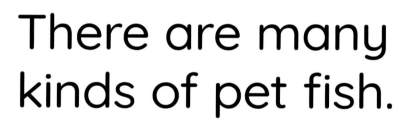

betta

clownfish

goldfish

Care

Pet fish live
in tanks.
Rocks cover
the bottom.

tank

Fish need the right water. Water is salty or **fresh**.

freshwater

Fish need clean water. **Filters** help keep water clean.

filter

Tanks get dirty. **Owners** clean the tank.

owner ↗

15

Fish eat **flakes** of food.

flakes

Fish like tanks with objects. Objects make it fun to swim!

object

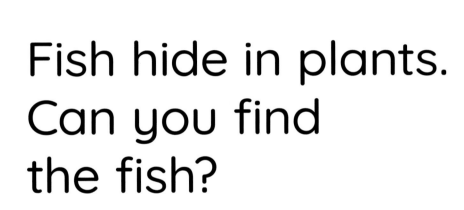

Fish hide in plants.
Can you find
the fish?

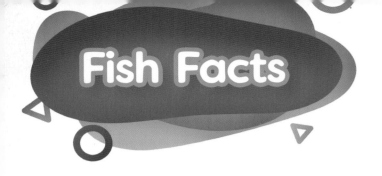

Fish Facts

Pet Fish Supplies

tank

filter

plants

rocks

flakes

Tank Objects

plants   castles   statues

Glossary

filters

tools that
clean water

flakes

small pieces
of food

fresh

water that is
not salty, like in
lakes or rivers

owners

people who
care for fish

To Learn More

ON THE WEB

FACTSURFER

Factsurfer.com gives you a safe, fun way to find more information.

1. Go to www.factsurfer.com.

2. Enter "pet fish" into the search box and click 🔍.

3. Select your book cover to see a list of related content.

Index